RHODE ISLAND

Helen Lepp Friesen

www.av2books.com

AV² provides enriched content that supplements and complements this book. Weigl's AV² books strive to create inspired learning and engage young minds in a total learning experience.

Your AV² Media Enhanced books come alive with...

Go to www.av2books.com, and enter this book's unique code.

BOOK CODE

N650445

AV² by Weigl brings you media enhanced books that support active learning.

Audio
Listen to sections of the book read aloud.

Key Words
Study vocabulary, and complete a matching word activity.

Video
Watch informative video clips.

Quizzes
Test your knowledge.

Embedded Weblinks
Gain additional information for research.

Slide Show
View images and captions, and prepare a presentation.

Try This!
Complete activities and hands-on experiments.

... and much, much more!

Published by AV² by Weigl
350 5th Avenue, 59th Floor
New York, NY 10118
Website: www.av2books.com   www.weigl.com

Library of Congress Cataloging-in-Publication Data
Friesen, Helen Lepp, 1961-
 Rhode Island / Helen Lepp Friesen.
   p. cm. -- (Explore the U.S.A.)
 Audience: Grades K-3.
 Includes bibliographical references and index.
 ISBN 978-1-61913-399-0 (hbk. : alk. paper)
 1. Rhode Island--Juvenile literature. I. Title.
 F79.3.F75 2013
 974.5--dc23
                        2012015939

Printed in the United States of America in North Mankato, Minnesota
1 2 3 4 5 6 7 8 9 16 15 14 13 12

052012
WEP040512

Project Coordinator: Karen Durrie
Art Director: Terry Paulhus

Weigl acknowledges Getty Images as the primary image supplier for this title.

2

RHODE ISLAND

Contents

3

This is Rhode Island.
It is called the Ocean State.
Rhode Island is next to the Atlantic Ocean.

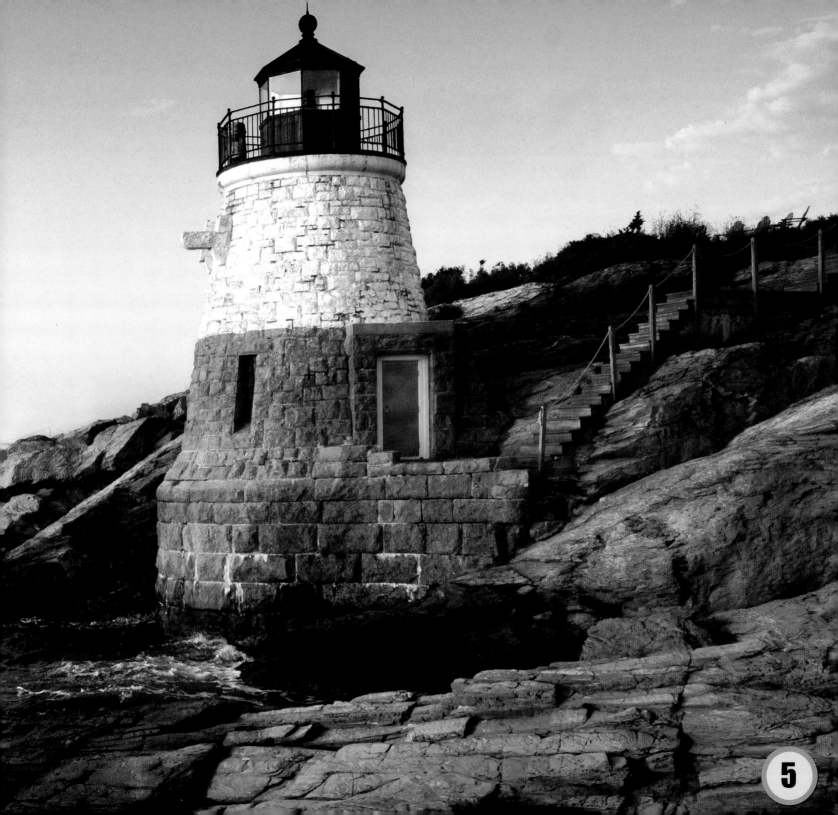

This is the shape of Rhode Island. It is in the east part of the United States. Rhode Island has 36 islands.

Where is Rhode Island?

Canada

W N E S

Pacific Ocean

United States

Atlantic Ocean

Mexico

Rhode Island is next to the Atlantic Ocean and two states.

Roger Williams led the first settlers to Rhode Island in 1636. He wanted to live in a place where people were free to believe what they want.

Roger Williams made friends with the American Indians in Rhode Island.

The violet is the Rhode Island state flower. School children voted to make the violet the state flower.

The Rhode Island state seal has a gold anchor and the state motto.

The anchor has stood for Rhode Island since 1636.

This is the state flag of Rhode Island. It is white, blue, and gold. It has 13 gold stars.

The stars stand for Rhode Island as the 13th state.

The Rhode Island Red chicken is the state bird. It has a red comb on its head. It is one of the most common chickens in the United States.

Rhode Island Red chickens lay brown eggs.

This is the biggest city in Rhode Island. It is called Providence. It is the state capital.

Providence has one of the oldest zoos in the United States.

People like to fish in the ocean by Rhode Island. They use boats to fish for cod, lobster, and striped bass.

Rhode Island makes $160 million each year from people who go saltwater fishing.

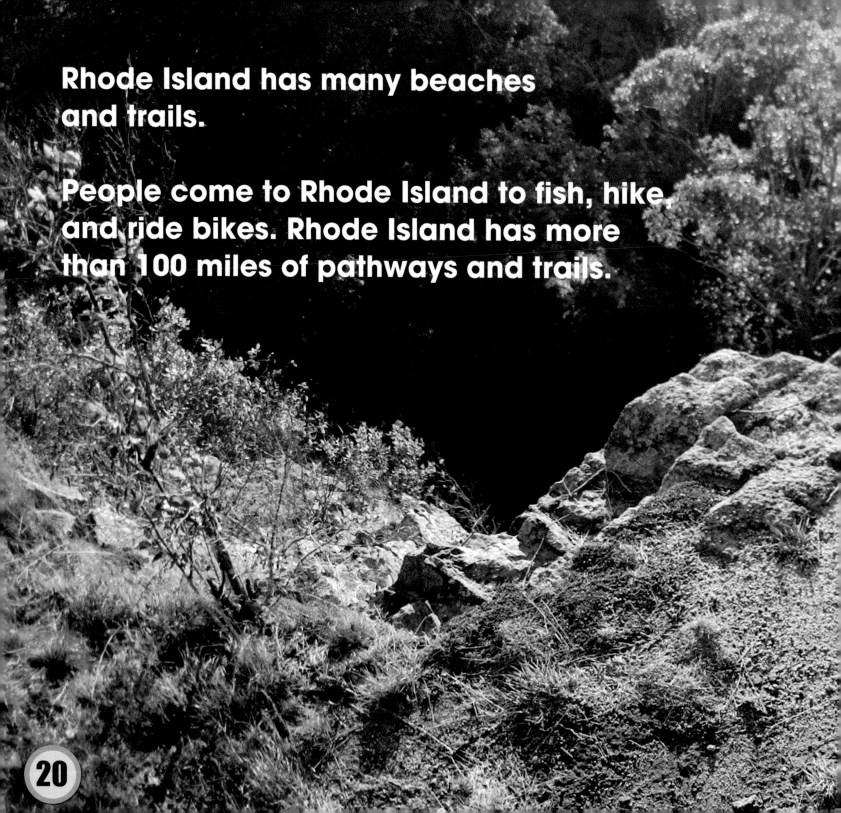

Rhode Island has many beaches and trails.

People come to Rhode Island to fish, hike, and ride bikes. Rhode Island has more than 100 miles of pathways and trails.

RHODE ISLAND FACTS

These pages provide detailed information that expands on the interesting facts found in the book. These pages are intended to be used by adults as a learning support to help young readers round out their knowledge of each state in the *Explore the U.S.A.* series.

Pages 4–5

Rhode Island is the smallest state in the United States. It is called the Ocean State because it is next to the Atlantic Ocean. Rhode Island has more than 400 miles (644 kilometers) of coastline. This includes the coasts of the bays and islands. The biggest bay is called Narragansett Bay. Rhode Island is sometimes called Little Rhody because of its size.

Pages 6–7

On May 29, 1790, Rhode Island became the 13th state to join the United States. Rhode Island borders Massachusetts and Connecticut. The state has two regions. These are the New England Uplands and the Coastal Lowlands. The Uplands are hilly. Rhode Island's 36 islands and many coastlines are part of the Coastal Lowlands, which are made up of sand dunes, beaches, and rocky cliffs.

Pages 8–9

Roger Williams was a pastor and teacher. He left Massachusetts because his beliefs were different and not accepted there. Along with others that shared his views, he moved to Rhode Island and bought land from American Indians there. The settlers named their new settlement Providence. Soon, other settlers who were looking for religious freedom arrived.

Pages 10–11

In 1897, the schoolchildren of Rhode Island voted the violet the state flower. This was not made official until 1968. The state seal has "Rhode Island and Providence Plantations" written around the edge. This is the official name of the state. The smallest state has the longest name.

Pages 12–13

The 13 stars on the flag represent the original 13 colonies and Rhode Island as the 13th state. The word "hope" on the blue ribbon underneath the anchor is the state motto. Hope was chosen from the Bible verse "hope we have as an anchor of the soul."

Pages 14–15

In 1954, the Rhode Island Red chicken was named the state bird. Rhode Island Red chickens are excellent egg producers. They begin laying eggs at four months old. The Rhode Island Red is one of the oldest chicken breeds in the United States.

Pages 16–17

Providence is located on the northern tip of Narragansett Bay. From 1854 to 1900, Rhode Island had two capitals, Newport and Providence. In 1900, Providence was named the only capital. One of the oldest zoos in the United States is the Roger Williams Park Zoo. It attracts more than 700,000 people each year.

Pages 18–19

Major industries in Rhode Island include fishing, farming, tourism, and manufacturing. Recreational saltwater fishing attracts many people. They spend money to charter boats and buy fishing gear in the state. Recreational saltwater fishing makes more money for the state than its commercial fisheries.

Pages 20–21

Tourism is a top industry in Rhode Island. People come to the state to go sailing, fishing, hiking, and cycling. Block Island has beautiful beaches. There is an extensive network of bike pathways in Rhode Island. Bicycle tours take people past beaches, villages, countrysides, and historic sites.

KEY WORDS

Research has shown that as much as 65 percent of all written material published in English is made up of 300 words. These 300 words cannot be taught using pictures or learned by sounding them out. They must be recognized by sight. This book contains 52 common sight words to help young readers improve their reading fluency and comprehension. This book also teaches young readers several important content words, such as proper nouns. These words are paired with pictures to aid in learning and improve understanding.

Page	Sight Words First Appearance
4	is, it, next, state, the, this, to
7	and, has, in, of, part, two, where
8	a, American, first, he, Indians, live, made, people, place, they, want, were, what, with
11	children, for, make, school
12	as, white
15	head, its, most, on, one
16	city
19	each, from, go, like, use, who, year
20	come, many, miles, more, than

Page	Content Words First Appearance
4	Atlantic Ocean, ocean, Rhode Island
7	islands, shape, United States
8	friends, Roger Williams, settlers
11	anchor, flower, seal, violet
12	flag, stars
15	bird, chicken, comb, eggs,
16	capital, Providence, zoos
19	boats, cod, lobster, striped bass
20	beaches, bikes, pathways, trails

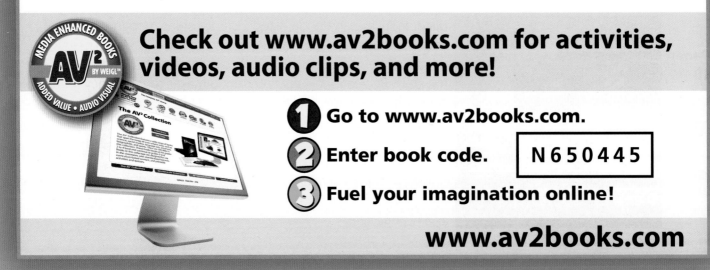

Check out www.av2books.com for activities, videos, audio clips, and more!

1 Go to www.av2books.com.

2 Enter book code. | N 6 5 0 4 4 5 |

3 Fuel your imagination online!

www.av2books.com